"Linda Martinson gives an eloquent voice to those who are deep in the experience of chronic pain and, in addition, she offers a means of empathy to those of us who have yet to experience that depth of pain. *Poetry of Pain* is an important expression of the experience of chronic pain."

> — William R.B. Anderson, Ph.D. with Jesse F. Taylor, Ph.D., co-authors of Chronic Pain: Taking Command Of Our Healing, New Energy Press

"If pain be considered the Destroyer of Souls, and
Poetry the window to one's soul,
then Linda Martinson's collection
presents us with a unique opportunity
to witness an individual's struggle for survival.

Patients with chronic pain will undoubtedly see their reflection in the delicate window Ms. Martinson reveals."

> —Mark Stillman, M.D., Washington State Cancer Pain Initiative, Medical Director, Hospice of Seattle

Also by Linda Martinson:
Simply Salmon: Fresh, Frozen & Canned
Simply Shrimp: Fresh, Frozen & Canned

Attention Organizations:
Most titles carried by Simply Books are available at special quantity discounts to volume buyers.

For details, contact the
Special Markets Department,
Simply Books
P. O. Box 2205
Lynnwood, WA 98036

BY LINDA MARTINSON

SIMPLY BOOKS • LYNNWOOD, WA

> If you purchased this book without a cover, you should be aware that it is stolen property. It was reported as "unsold and destroyed" to the publisher, and neither the author nor the publisher has received any payment for this "stripped" book.

No part of this book may be reproduced or transmitted in any form or by any means, electronic or mechanical, including photocopying, recording, or by any information storage and retrieval system, without written permission from the Publisher, except by a reviewer who may quote brief passages in a review to be printed in a magazine or newspaper.

Poetry of Pain
Copyright © 1996 by Linda Martinson
All Rights Reserved

Design by Beverly Theunis

ISBN: 0-9648978-2-2

Library of Congress Catalog Card Number: 95-92651

Manufactured in the United States of America

10 9 8 7 6 5 4 3 2 1

Simply Books
P.O. Box 2205
Lynnwood, WA 98036

"To write poetry is to risk emotion;
to read poetry is to understand."

"Pain nourishes courage. You can't be brave if you've only had wonderful things happen to you."

—*Mary Tyler Moore*

Contents

Forward   xi
Preface   xiii
Acknowledgements   xvi
Wading Through The Words   1
Morning Ritual   2
Bad Days Are No Fun At All   4
War Crimes   5
Giving In   6
I Wish I Was A Cat   8
Vanilla Pain   9
Love Vs. Peace   10
Supermarket Concessions   12
To The People Who've Never Lived With Chronic Pain But Like To Give Free Advice   13
Comfortable People   14
On Realizing That Anger Is Wasted Energy   17
Boiled Over Again   18
Old Faithful   19
Where's The Birthday Girl?   20

CONTENTS

Circus Gal   22

Where Do I Sign Up
For More Good Days?   24

The Yearning   26

Love Poem   28

Mantra   29

Breaking Through   30

SOUL TALK

   I.   Acceptance   32

   II.   Metamorphosis   34

ON LIVING WITH CHRONIC PAIN

   I.   Dark Times   36

   II.   Illumination   37

Cataract Canyon, Utah   38

Your Thoughts   39

Directory of Chronic Pain Associations   41

Forward

My late grandfather, a pediatrician, would say about some childhood ailments: "they won't kill you; you'll just wish you were dead." Were he alive today, he would most certainly describe fibromyalgia this way. As sufferers know, fibromyalgia causes diffuse pain and fatigue. Yet, because individuals with this problem appear normal in all respects, fibromyalgia does not get the full attention due such a potentially disabling disorder. In fact, the average person with fibromyalgia goes undiagnosed for at least five years. To make matters worse, people with this medical condition are not complainers. They are generally hard workers who do not share their symptoms with colleagues or even friends. Thus, non-sufferers will often brush aside complaints because not only do persons with fibromyalgia look normal, but they often function normally. All of this applied to a condition which may be more disabling than even rheumatoid arthritis, according to the published literature.

What has helped the recognition of this condition the most has been the formation of support groups. For the first time, individuals with this disorder have united for political, educational, and therapeutic benefits. These support groups have been instrumental in effecting public recognition, insurance reform and additional research funding. Individuals with fibromyalgia, as first described centuries ago by

Poetry of Pain

Socrates, are definitely "survivors."

Linda Martinson, the author of this fine collection of poetry, is one such survivor. Linda had never even heard of fibromyalgia until an automobile collision eight years ago. Instead of healing over time, she became much worse and failed to get appropriate medical therapy since her pain "did not show up on an x-ray or in blood tests." Like most sufferers with fibromyalgia, she was initially filled with self-doubt as others told her it was "in her head." Only through persistence was she finally diagnosed only to discover there is no cure for this condition whose etiology is unknown. Linda has continued to function despite sometimes overwhelming symptoms and with an appreciation for her profound limitations.

This book is deeply moving. It's an encyclopedia for fibromyalgia sufferers —or any pain sufferer—who will recognize and empathize with almost every word. It's also about determination, hope and empowerment. If there were such a designation as Poet Laureate of Pain, Linda Martinson would surely bear the title.

—*Paul B. Brown, MD. PhD*
Seattle, Washington

Paul B. Brown, MD, PhD practices rheumatology in Seattle where he is a Clinical Associate Professor at the University of Washington. He is the author of a number of scholarly articles and has appeared on a weekly television show, "Healthtalk," on PBS.

Preface

We writers are told, "Write what you know." I know about pain.

Eight years ago I was in a head-on car wreck. No bones were broken; I just hurt. I waited, as most people do, for my body to heal. Doesn't it always? The accident occurred while I was touring with my first cookbook, *Simply Salmon: Fresh, Frozen & Canned*, and finishing up the manuscript for *Simply Shrimp*. Still, I managed to complete my second book on schedule before leaving for Egypt to study Middle Eastern dance.

Over time, my pain intensified and spread to every part of my body. Sleep was impossible. Yet, none of the doctors or specialists I consulted could tell me why. It's a pity pain doesn't show on an x-ray or in blood tests, for, lacking "proof" of pain or knowledge of the cause of my condition, I was treated, for the most part, like a malingerer. Several doctors dismissed me with, "You're over 40 — you're bound to have some aches and pains!"

I went to a sports medicine clinic only to be told by the head physician, "Football players get back on the field in two weeks — why didn't you?" I felt betrayed, bewildered, angry, and secretly doubted my sanity as I struggled to remember words. I could barely function through the pain which engulfed me day and night. My family suffered, my career

PREFACE

suffered, and I was further devastated when a physical therapist ordered me to give up my dancing, the source of so much joy.

Finally, four years after the accident, a Seattle physician diagnosed me with a chronic musculoskeletal pain and fatigue disorder called *fibromyalgia*. I was elated; now that I had a name for my condition I could be cured! Then came deep despair upon learning that the cure for fibromyalgia (FM) has yet to be discovered.

How did I contract this disease? My FM was triggered by the car accident.

I'm grateful to my doctor for urging me to join the Seattle Fibromyalgia Association (now renamed The Seattle Fibromyalgia International Team), a support group that has helped me to accept my disease, learn how to best live with it, and determine safe and reasonable treatment approaches. I continue to do research, and try a multitude of medications and therapies in an attempt to control my symptoms. Knowledge is power, and I've come to realize that I don't have to apologize to anyone for my pain anymore.

Chronic pain sufferers are not alone. If you would like to learn more about support organizations, please consult the directory in the back of this book.

PREFACE

I find great solace in poetry; when my pain is at its height I feel especially driven to express it on paper. (It's actually easier to write when the pain is driving me crazy; there's no left brain editor getting in the way of what I want to say.) After the poem is written I feel cleansed, even satisfied.

This book, then, is a walk through the phases of chronic pain I've come to know so well: frustration, fear, anger, depression, acknowledgement, acceptance and hope.

Acknowledgements

This book is dedicated to my husband Don, our sons, Matt and Andy, and the rest of my family: thank you for helping me through the tough times and the everyday stuff. Words of encouragement and love to Andy and my sister Tammy, who know the pain of migraine headaches, and to Matt, who has inherited more than my good sense of humor. Love and kisses to my mother, whose encouragement keeps me writing, and who cheers me up with flowers and her credit card.

This book is also dedicated to my long-time friend Diane Cederstrand who, suffering from Sjögren's Syndrome, can't cry because she doesn't have any tears, and to my dear friend Patricia Hendricksen, founder of the Seattle Fibromyalgia International Team, who has saved my life more than once. Blessings to my long-distance friend Esfira Edelstein, who comforted me when I cried. To Jo Nelson, Writer-in-Residence for the Washington State Arts Commission: thank you for the valuable advice.

I'm indebted to Ralph Boragine, Executive Director of the American Seafood Institute and Publisher of the *ASI Report* (a publication for which I've been a columnist for the last five years). Thank you, Ralph, for your inspiration and many useful suggestions.

Poetry of Pain

All my life I've wanted to do something beautiful. I will always be grateful to Beverly Theunis, who, through her creative genius, generosity, and sincere appreciation of this project, has helped me to make this beautiful book.

I am deeply grateful to Linda Person, an instant friend who became an editor. Linda has fibromyalgia and she hurts as much as I do. She, too, knows the poetry of pain.

WADING THROUGH THE WORDS

Throbbing,
Burning,
Pounding,
Shooting,
Stabbing.
Ceaseless.
These words are flat
compared to the pain I feel.

There's an animal on my neck
and I can't shake it off.
The weight is heavy,
the teeth are sharp,
the claws dig in.

MORNING RITUAL

I'm sleeping soundly,
enjoying my dream,
when Old Bladder
(more reliable than my alarm clock)
wakes me up.
A glance at the time:
it's early ... too early!
If I don't get back to sleep
I'll lose the day.

Hurry to the bathroom,
hurry back to bed,
Hurry! Slip back into the dream.
Try not to panic,
though movement stirs the pain
like witch's brew.
Try to float away as
sharp spines in my feet
begin to pulse.
Pumping, pumping,
gaining momentum

with each heartbeat,
the explosion blisters up
through my legs,
through my hips.
It feels like the magician
really did cut the lady in half.

I'm trying to sleep.
I need my sleep!
But my neck feels like
someone smashed it with a hammer;
the burning in my hands
resonates
like a Tibetan bell.

I burrow beneath the quilt,
desperate to re-enter my dream world.
But it's gone,
and Reality takes its place:
It hurts too much to lay here.
Time to get up.

Poetry of Pain

BAD DAYS ARE NO FUN AT ALL

On The Bad Days
I just try to exist.
I try to cope;
I try to be.

The Bear is back,
demanding full attention;
claws ripping,
spittle burning;
hungry for meat.

Oh, the hot baths,
the heat rubs,
the desperate meditations
may lessen the roar
for a moment or two,
but they don't change the facts.

Yellow eyes gleam watchful,
ready to complete the charge.

I have no place to hide.

WAR CRIMES

The chronic pain that rages
through my flesh
tatoos my soul.
I long for a final solution.

My body is a
concentration camp
where tortures abound;
persecutions
that should never be condoned
by any society.
A broken spirit
with slow, sad eyes
dwells within.
Passion gone.
Hope gone.
Heart-cries beg for release;
heart-ashes powder my bones.

GIVING IN

My face is wet with pain.
I took a bath tonight;
didn't want to —
fought it.
Hey!
I just showered this morning!
But the demons in my muscles wouldn't stop.
Had to have their way;
wouldn't be ignored.

Sometimes, when they gang up,
they overcome me.
I know a bath will send them
scuttling to their dens ...
temporarily.
Still I resist.

Poetry of Pain

Too busy. Miss Perfect.
But it's more than that:
I want to have the strength to fight their fire.
This rape,
This violation
robs me of my charge ...
degrades my soul.

I immerse my body into the hot,
churning waters of my bath
and I allow the primal sounds to come out.
This must be
how the ancient Egyptian women sounded
when they wailed for the dead.

I WISH I WAS A CAT

I wish I was a cat,
snoozing in a rocking chair,
waiting for dinner.

I wish I was a cat,
lying on the floor,
warming in the sun.

A full stomach.
No obligations.
Always the boss.

I wish I was a cat
— a *healthy* cat!

VANILLA PAIN

He put some salts into my bath.
Vanilla scented, they were;
heat dulls pain.
He lit a candle.
Vanilla scented, it was;
Perfume soothes injured senses.

I told him
I would put all my pain
into the lone bubble
floating on the water.
I said
it would never burst.
And then ...

I lay in the water,
crying,
letting him see for the first time
the mask of tragedy that
became,
but did not become,
my face.

Poetry of Pain

LOVE VS. PEACE

Okay, folks, what'll it be today?
Should I throw myself off a bridge,
or should I cook dinner?
Everyone's depending on me
and I hate it.

It would be easier to deal with this pain
if I were the only one I had to consider.
I'm sick of it —
and still I go on.
Why?

Would it be a sin to kill myself?
I don't think so.
It's a sin to hurt so much;
the raven sitting on my neck
becomes impatient.

Poetry of Pain

I have my husband,
my children who love me.
Would doing the deed hurt them
more than I already hurt myself?
It's a toss up.

But wait, let's think about this.
Does the pain in my body
supersede a grieving heart?
I am surrounded by love —
yet right now —
love doesn't supersede the pain.

Thank God it isn't always this intense
or I would have to leave them.

SUPERMARKET CONCESSIONS

I am paying for my groceries
at the check stand.
"How ya doin?" he asks.
I look at his eyes, tempted
to startle him with the truth.
But he doesn't really want to know.
So I opt for a nice, neutral,
bland word that means nothing.
A fat word that fills the mouth.
"Fine," I say to his shoulder,
"I'm doin' just fine."

Poetry of Pain

TO THE PEOPLE WHO'VE NEVER LIVED WITH CHRONIC PAIN BUT LIKE TO GIVE FREE ADVICE

When you tell me you want to cut off your arms
with a meat cleaver,
When you dream you've cut off your leg at the knee
and wrapped it in waxed paper
so you won't bloody the sheets,
When your head is packed
with angry slivers of glass,
Will you *still* preach to me
about how you just ignore
your aches and pains?

COMFORTABLE PEOPLE

Comfortable people
living comfortable lives
go home to their
comfortable dreams.
They comfortably tell me
to live with my pain;
it's all in my head,
so it seems.

When I beg for relief,
my comfortable doctors and
comfortable nurses are curt.
*You can't take narcotics
for pain,*
they explain.
*They're reserved
for patients who hurt!*

Go home and put up your feet,
they advise.
*Get a life,
you hyper-dramatic.*

I can't feel your pain,
I won't feel your pain
(and besides,
you might be an addict!)

Give no credence to studies
that refute drug abuse
when the user is
in chronic pain.
Remember,
I have a degree.
(And besides,
you look fine to me.)

How dare you ask
to be functional?
That's reserved
for people like me.
"Quality of Life"
is a term that's reserved
for intelligent people
like me.

Poetry of Pain

More health professionals need to become sensitive to the special needs of chronic pain patients. And it is true that some doctors who refuse to prescribe adequate pain relief are fearful of criticism by their peers and state medical boards. There is a growing movement, however, toward the more compassionate and humane treatment of intractable pain. (According to California State Senate Bill No. 1402, "Intractable pain," ... means a pain state in which the cause of the pain cannot be removed or otherwise treated and which in the generally accepted course of medical practice no relief or cure of the cause of the pain is possible or none has been found after reasonable efforts including, ... evaluation by the attending physician and surgeon and one or more physicians and surgeons specializing in the treatment of the area, system, or organ of the body perceived as the source of the pain.)

At this printing, several states have enacted statutes, guidelines, and policy statements which protect physicians from disciplinary action by their respective boards for prescribing controlled substances in the course of treatment of a patient with intractable pain.

ON REALIZING THAT ANGER IS WASTED ENERGY

I can be bitter and mean
OR I can drop it.
It's my choice.
I can work at this illness,
learn what I can,
do what I can for myself,
OR I can be bitter and mean.
It's my choice.

BOILED OVER AGAIN

I do my best to keep the pot simmering,
but it's boiled over again.

I'm a reasonable patient —
I listen.
I meditate,
I exercise,
I eat right
(most of the time).
I apply the hot packs,
I apply the cold packs;
I take the pills.
Still it's boiled over again.

It's tough to live with a disease
for which there is no cure
because we don't know the cause.
Yet I guess I could
look at it this way:
At least the pot hasn't boiled dry.

OLD FAITHFUL

I wish I could blame them all on the pain
(my struggles).
But self-delusion is a coward's tool.
Life wasn't exactly perfect
before I got this disease.
Is it ever?

Sometimes, the ache in my body
is a distraction
for my sad heart.
Comforting.
Always there.
More reliable than people
who desert my love.

Poetry of Pain

WHERE'S THE BIRTHDAY GIRL?

Today is my birthday.
I feel old.
Achy.
Exhausted.
Vain enough to resent the
stress lines around my eyes.
(Oh, I know some of this comes with age —
but not all of it.)

It's as though I'm black and white
in a black and white world.
I've tried so many different medications
yet I can't seem to gain any color.
Once,
after taking something for pain,
my body was tinged with pastels
that faded as quickly as they came.

Poetry of Pain

Today is my birthday.
I'm going to celebrate by going to the doctor.
Getting stuck in rush hour traffic —
both ways.
But you know what?
I'm going to do my darndest
to make this a pastel kind of day.

Poetry of Pain

CIRCUS GAL

Every day I perform
my circus act;
I'm the gal who balances
several spinning plates
at a time while the crowd
looks on in astonishment.
Watch in wonder as I
pirouette a platter of pain
on my left hand.
Dexterous digits
hold it as far away
from my body as possible.
With astounding concentration
I balance a whirling dish
of sanity upon my head;
can't drop this one.
Be amazed as I revolve
a plateful of family
obligations on the
perfectly poised fingers
of my right hand.

How does she do it?
But wait — there's more!
On my right knee spins
yet another plate:
a career!
Ta da!
And what's this?
Circus Gal is attempting to
twirl a saucer of spare time
on her left knee!
What a show!

But I need a little
help from the audience.
Any volunteers?
I have to relegate
and delegate
so I can concentrate.
Gotta try to equalize
the size of these plates
before they crash.

Poetry of Pain

WHERE DO I SIGN UP
FOR MORE GOOD DAYS?

Some days are better than others.
On those days
I GET THINGS DONE!

The work piles up
when you don't feel well.
Dusty window sills,
lines unwritten,
paperwork scattered on the floor.
A call to the in-laws
to thank them for the crab.

On the good days
I get things done.
The trick is not to overdo it,
or the next day
is pay-day.
Though sometimes,
(just between you and me)
it's worth it.

Like when I give
a dance performance
and aggravate my shoulder:
At least I heard the music;
some people never do.
At least I danced.

Actually,
I'm kind of proud of myself.
It would be so easy to quit.
But I won't.

THE YEARNING

I used to go to sleep
with my head
on his shoulder.
I'd curl into the
hollows of his body
and he'd read to me
from a book
just boring enough.
Oh, how I miss the
intimacies of love!
The prickly outline
of his beard
undulating in the lamplight
as his lips formed words,
the gentle sound vibration
that tickled my hand
as it lay upon his chest,
the soft distraction
of his cheekbone
waiting for my kiss.

Poetry of Pain

Pain,
Oh Wicked Pain,
must you steal this from me too?
Must you dictate
every aspect of my life?
Let me lay
as lovers lie
without your insidious presence,
my head upon his shoulder
once again.

Poetry of Pain

LOVE POEM

If you hurt, give this poem to someone you love, to the one who cares for you. I gave mine to my husband. If you're handling your pain on your own, please give this poem to yourself.

Your favors are like flowers,
bright spots of color in my life.
Your compassion is as constant
as the pain in my body.
A touch,
a look,
to be held when I hurt;
these gifts are as important as food.
You nourish my soul,
and for this,
I love you.

MANTRA

My heart follows the sunbeams
to the place of light
where all is serene.
Where the colors are brilliant,
and the tree bears apples
and blossoms at the same time.
I am at peace;
I understand.

Sometimes, when the pain is bad, I need to be someplace else. Out of my body, just for a little while. Mantra *is based on the near death experience my husband had as a child.*

Poetry of Pain

BREAKING THROUGH

How do you know
unless you've been there?
I know.
I know the hopelessness;
the frustration;
the agony;
the total isolation.

And I know
the exhilaration
of breaking through
those barriers to learn
the Truth.
There is a reason:
I'm part of The Plan.
I am here to love
and help others.
The pain is the means.

SOUL TALK

Poetry of Pain

1. ACCEPTANCE

I get so frustrated when I want to work
and I can't because my body fails me.
I grieve for the energy I used to have,
for the days when I would erupt out of bed,
ready to go.

Lost times.
Lost life.

I miss the spontaneity of good health,
when I could do simple things,
like go for a drive,
or dance,
without having to consider the toll
on my body.
I miss the fun.

ON LIVING WITH CHRONIC PAIN

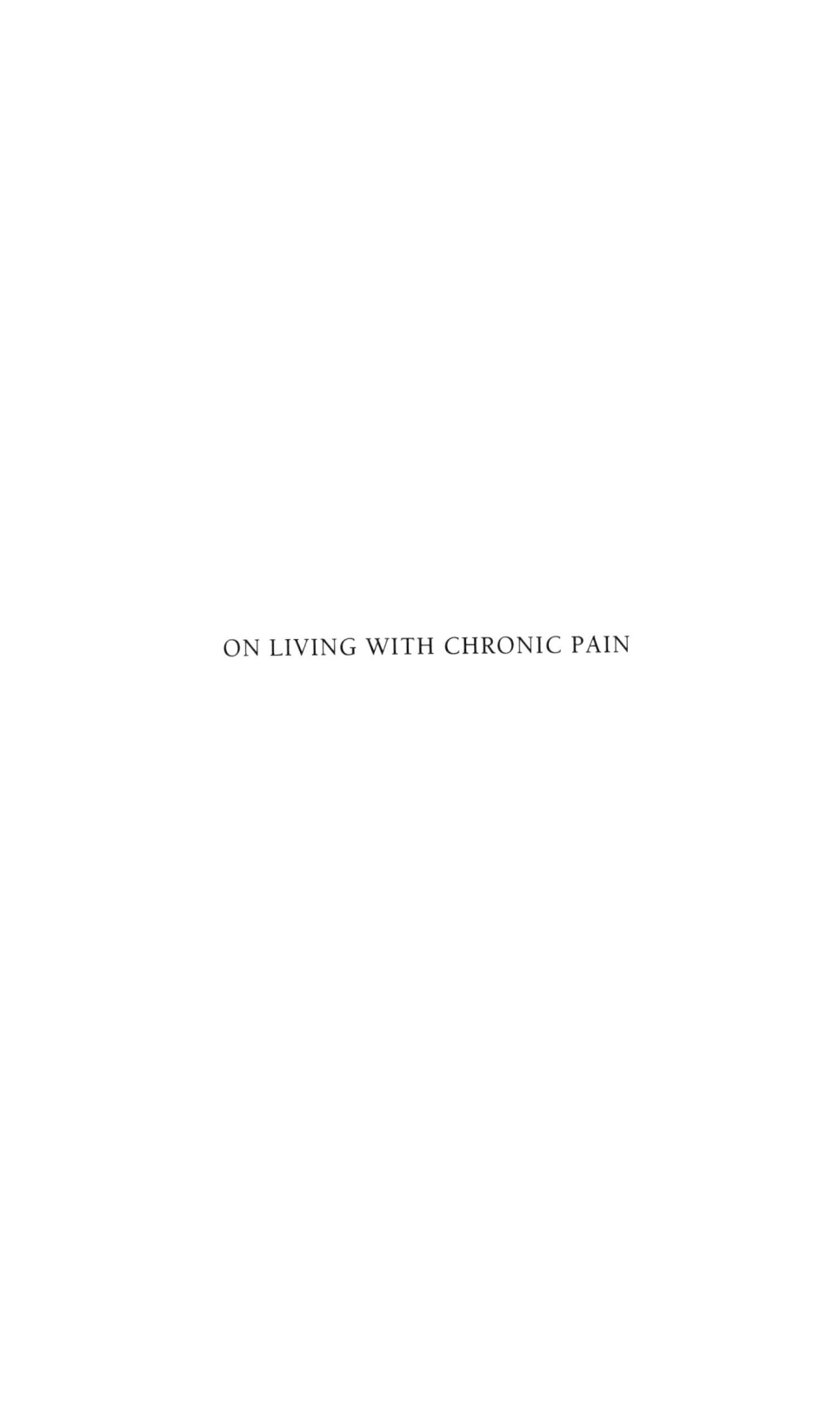

Poetry of Pain

I. DARK TIMES

I am awash with pain, my tyranny.
It covers me like seaweed,
clinging, stinking;
the salt is in my wounds.

Searing my muscles with perpetual passion,
pain invades my mind,
my privacy.
Afraid I am drowning
when I so want to live,
I cry.

II. ILLUMINATION

Savor life as though you are sucking on a lemon drop.
Revel in the tartness;
let it lead you to the sweet.

A lemon drop is Now!

Be in the Present Moment,
tasting each experience;
not reliving past illness
or exaggerating health's future.

For life,
like a lemon drop,
is soon over,
and it is good to have enjoyed it.

CATARACT CANYON, UTAH

Pink flowers
on a dry desert bush;
survivors,
just like me.

The petals of the sun
reach down to touch me.
A cool breeze blows,
nuzzling my senses,
waking them up.

Surrounded by cliffs
layered like
Neapolitan cookies;
brick red,
chocolate purple,
and alabaster.
Crenelated monuments
gifted to the sky.

I am alive.

Poetry of Pain

YOUR THOUGHTS ...

Poetry of Pain

YOUR THOUGHTS ...

DIRECTORY OF CHRONIC PAIN ASSOCIATIONS

American Chronic Pain Association
P.O. Box 850
Rocklin, CA 95677
(916) 632-0922

American Juvenile Arthritis Organization
1314 Spring St. N.W.
Atlanta, GA 30309
(404) 872-7100

Arthritis Foundation
1314 Spring St. N.W.
Atlanta, GA 30309
(404) 872-7100
(800) 283-7800

Fibromyalgia Association of British Columbia
P.O. Box 15455,
Vancouver, B.C.
Canada
V6B5B2
(604) 739-3905

Poetry of Pain

Fibromyalgia Network
P.O. Box 31750
Tucson, AZ 85751-1750
(602) 290-5508
(800) 853-2929

National Chronic Pain
Outreach Association
7979 Old Georgetown Road, Suite 100
Bethesda, MD 20814-2429
(301) 652-4948

National Committee On
The Treatment of Intractable Pain
c/o Wayne Coy Jr., President
Cohn and Marks
1333 New Hampshire Ave. N.W.
Washington, D.C. 20036

National Headache Foundation
5252 North Western Ave.
Chicago, IL 60625
(312) 878-7715
(800) 843-2256

Pain Ministries
932 Industry Drive
Building No. 24
Tukwila, WA 98188
(206) 575-3335

Seattle Fibromyalgia
International Team, Inc.
P.O. Box 77373
Seattle, WA 98177-0373
(206) 362-2310

The CFIDS Association of America, Inc.
P.O. Box 220398
Charlotte, NC 28222-0398
(800) 442-3437
(900) 896-2343

Washington Intractable / Chronic
Pain Advocacy
2308 N.E. 23rd Avenue
Vancouver, WA 98665
(360) 574-0467
(503) 223-8640

THE AUTHOR

Photo by Karen Moskowitz

Linda Martinson lives in the Pacific Northwest with her family. She is the author of two seafood cookbooks, a trade magazine columnist, and performer of Middle Eastern cabaret belly dance. Linda has suffered the chronic pain of Fibromyalgia constantly since 1987, and helped to write the guidelines for Washington State's *Task Force on Policies for Management of Chronic Intractable Pain.*